DON'T INSIST ON DYING

DON'T INSIST ON DYING

APPLYING THE LESSONS OF BIBLE HEROES WHO NEVER DIED

BY DANIEL G. STOCKIN

Published by Pioneer Place Ministries Inc.
P.O. Box 1051 Ellijay GA 30540 USA

Email: office@pioneerinsights.org

More information about Pioneer Place Ministries
can be found at www.pioneerinsights.org

This book is for entertainment purposes only. It is the opinion of the writer. It is not to be construed as medical advice. The consequences of how readers think, speak, and act after reading the information in this book are born solely by the readers. In all we do, we must act wisely, not impulsively, foolishly, or devoid of respect for others.

© 2021 Daniel G. Stockin

All rights reserved. No part of this book may be copied, scanned, reproduced in any way, or stored in a retrieval system or transmitted in any form or by any means, electronic, mechanical, photocopying, recording, or otherwise, without obtaining the written permission of the publisher. Contact the publisher for information about efforts to make the book available in different languages.

Initial publication 2021.

ISBN 978-0-9720029-1-2 (paperback)
ISBN 978-0-9720029-2-9 (ePub)

DEDICATION

Two things I have experienced have shown me that nothing is impossible to me, a simple man of no particular station or gifts. All I've ever really had to offer is my heart. But the two things have given me a knowing that a third will happen. This book is dedicated to the One that saw my heart and manifested the first two, and will just as certainly manifest the third.

DISCLAIMER

This book is for entertainment purposes only. It is the opinion of the writer. It is not to be construed as medical advice. The consequences of how readers think, speak, and act after reading the information in this book are born solely by the readers. In all we do, we must act wisely, not impulsively, foolishly, or devoid of respect for others.

CONTENTS

Dedication iii
Disclaimer iv
Preface 1
Chapters
1 Does Something Seem "Off" In What You've Been Told About God, Death and The Bible? 5
2 If You Wish to be Truly Free, How Can You Argue for Your Own Death? 13
3 It Is Scriptural, That We Can Conquer Death 17
4 Inconvenient Lazarus 31
5 The Questions We Must Each Answer After Reading the "Life, Not Death" Verses 37
6 About "Sinning" and Being "Appointed Once to Die" 43
7 The Formless God, and Saving Your House 55
8 Obtaining a Testimony that You Please God 61
9 About Your "Ascension" and Your New Body 69
10 Avoiding Death, for the UnBibled 75
11 The Conclusion of the Matter 83
Connecting with Others Who Resonate with This Message, and Supporting Its Spread 88

PREFACE

ABOUT PARROTS, THIS BOOK, AND THE PEOPLE WHO READ IT

What do parrots have to do with a book about not dying? Well, parrots are the reason it has taken so long for a book such as this to be written.

For a very long time, like the bird that mimics sounds, people have parroted others' words and ideas about God, life and death without having true *understanding* of what is being said. The words they parrot typically come from someone they believe should be trusted. Through repetition the teachings become comfortable and familiar, but they are still only vaguely thought through by most who adopt them. The ideas and doctrines are frequently passed down for generations, being accepted by most without an understanding of the biases, ignorance and error that framed them.

Whether you are a bible translator living 400 years ago, a church pastor today, or simply an average person seeking to understand "God," *no one should simply parrot the spiritual understandings of another.* Parroting others' ideas about God is what has gotten the world into the sad state it is in.

One of the common parroted teachings is that there are some things about God and our experiences that you should just accept as unknowable "until after you die and go to be with God." This makes no sense, when Jesus said that the Holy Spirit would "guide us into *all* truth." Being kept in a state of *guessing* also flies in the face of statements by the apostle Paul, who wrote in six places that he "would not have you be ignorant."

Another frequently parroted idea is that no one can be forever free from dying until *after* they die. Even bible teachers commonly say this, despite biblical accounts of Enoch and Elijah proving death is not a requirement for every person.

We must not accept doctrinal statements as true just because they are familiar, or because religious teachers promote them. **Make a note -- literally, make a note -- of every word or idea you don't understand, and ask God to give you understanding of the truth or fiction of it, and to give you the persistence and self-honesty required to gain the understanding you seek.**

God must speak to you, personally, bearing witness inside you as to what is true and what is false. Don't believe something any spiritual teacher, author, family member, bible scholar, or other person says, just because they say it. That includes this book. Know for yourself. Don't parrot others! *Parroting is the problem!*

This writing is for those who think deeply and are not comfortable with ignorance. It is not for those comfortable with drive-by spirituality, or for those unwilling to relook at what we've been taught previously. It is for those who have a nagging uneasiness about doctrines they have been taught, and for those whose contemplations have left them still seeking something more, something comprehensive, that explains ... everything. This book explains life and death, but also more than that. It explains the why ... of you.

The bible quotes in this book are taken from the King James Bible, not because it is necessarily the best translation, but because it is the one the Spirit has chosen to speak to the writer of this book through. All versions of the bible contain the fingerprints of biases and ignorance of the translators – perhaps more readily seen in some versions than others.

So with these things said, let's dive in.

Jesus said that the Truth will make you free.

Free from what?

Everything BUT dying?

CHAPTER 1

Does Something Seem "Off" In What You've Been Told About God, Death and The Bible?

Nobody wants to die. We're told by religious leaders that the message of the scriptures is that we can be delivered from death ... but not until *after* we die.

In the bible we read that two people named Enoch and Elijah left this earth without dying. But apparently they were special people, our teachers tell us: what happened to them doesn't happen for regular folks like you and me.

This book addresses the implications of what happened to Enoch and Elijah, that what they experienced can indeed happen to others who are alive, here and now, today. This writing dives into the bible verses that bear this out, many of which have not been examined in this light by those who study the bible.

Dropping your body to decay in the ground is something you have a say in, whether or not you know the bible. This is not to say that knowing what is in the scriptures is not a useful thing. In fact, when you have your eyes opened to this, you will find much confirmation in the scriptures that death to your physical frame is not mandatory.

Chapter 1

The time we are living in today is ushering in a higher understanding of the words of Jesus and the entire bible. **Presented in this book is a groundbreaking summary of bible verses about overcoming death, but after the bible teachings are addressed, we will also discuss avoiding death through understandings gained without referencing bible teachings.**

People rightfully have concerns about how parts of the bible have been translated, assembled and taught. Understanding the scriptures requires hearing from the Author of it, to nudge you where there are mistranslations or missing text, and show you where you are seeing the truths incorrectly. But if you have an internal knowing that the point of the biblical writings is for you to understand them and not remain in the state of guessing as to what is true, and if you believe that God is a fair God, equally available to all, you will want to consider the implications of what we read in the scriptures about avoiding death.

Everything that Jesus did and commanded his followers to do assists us in getting victory over "sin" and death (*sin* doesn't mean what you were taught it does). **This victory over death can occur before one's physical body dies -- eliminating death, not just postponing it.** This truth has been right there in front of us in the bible for centuries. It is now time for the Message of Life to be revealed, the Message that has always been there. The bible calls this Message **the Word of Life.**

If you are of an open heart, yearning for something you've always felt is somehow missing in our understanding of life, death, God and the bible, this is it.

About Cemeteries Outside Churches

You may have heard a statement something to this effect: Do what everyone else does, and you will get the results everyone else gets.

Not dying is certainly a different result. In the movies, in our culture, in our religious gatherings, it's very regularly depicted that dying is a noble thing. And of course, there are many people who die every day on our planet, and to their loved ones and often many others, they are indeed wonderful and inspiring people.

This is not in any way meant to be disrespectful to, or judgmental about people that have passed on. But let's be honest. Whether involved in religious endeavors or not, every man feels a resistance to death. It seems unfair. It appears to rule over us. It's jarring and often leaves behind people with severe depression or loneliness. In a statement of resigned exasperation or hopelessness, we say death is lumped-in with paying taxes as one of the two things we can't avoid.

Outside of many religious buildings are cemeteries where the bodies of many wonderful people are buried. But does it provide any real comfort, does it provide much to be excited about, that waiting just ahead of you is a diminishment of your bodily functions and then having your body join the other bodies in the dirt? Does it seem unfair, in light of reading the accounts of Enoch and Elijah and Jesus not experiencing death when they left this earth plane? Do well-manicured cemeteries somehow ring hollow, when we read that Jesus raised the dead, told and enabled others to go and raise the dead, and also said that all things are possible to him that believes?

Does it make sense to you that to obtain the different result of avoiding death, one must at least be open to exploring the concept? Does it make sense to you that the message of Jesus was not to teach mankind how to die, since man has been doing that quite successfully for a very long time? Could it be that the message of Jesus, and in fact the whole message of the bible, is that there is a way to be free that includes even being free from death?

Death happens quite regularly. One does not need to do anything special, it just ... happens. It doesn't require any special actions or knowledge. Just keep living the way people live, and it will occur with clock-like precision, because of what the apostle Paul called "the law of sin and death." **But if you wish to bypass death, you are required to think and do *something different*. The questions to ask are: What do I need to think and do differently, and am I willing to do that?**

There is a life-altering message in this writing, if you can receive it: The bible clearly tells us that we do not "need" to die.

Note that I'm not saying that a new message is being ushered in today, but rather that a new and higher *understanding of* the words of the bible is now coming forth. This higher understanding being made known to humanity is a fulfillment of the words of Daniel 12:4, where we see that at the time of the end "knowledge will be increased."

Most people think knowledge increasing means we as humans will know more about atoms, history, the stars, and all kinds of things. And of course, it does include that kind of "more" knowledge. But "increase" means more than this.

In John 16:13, Jesus tells us that when the Spirit of Truth has come, this Spirit "will guide you into *all* truth." But simply having "more" information (knowledge) isn't **all** truth. What we need is knowledge that has "increased" to become wisdom, and the wisdom "increased" to become understanding.

In the bible, the term "increase" means a manifestation of a new form or fruit – in this case, a new form of knowledge. All three (knowledge, wisdom, and understanding) are each a form of knowledge, but Understanding is the *greatest* form of knowledge. It is described in 1 Corinthians 13:9-10 as perfect (full, complete) knowing, "when that which is perfect is come." And it doesn't need to come in some far-off future. Understanding can come while you are still here on earth.

King Solomon spoke a great deal about the benefits of getting knowledge and wisdom, but also advised that "with all thy getting, get understanding" (Proverbs 4:7). Without understanding, one cannot live forever and not die. But eternal life CAN be your experience NOW, if you reach the place of Understanding.

The Seed, the Tree, and the Fruit

All truth is parallel, and in our discussion of knowledge, wisdom, and understanding, it is useful to look at the example of a seed, its tree, and the fruit of the tree. The seed that is dead and alone "dies" to its current form when it is buried in the earth, during which time it is quickened to become a living, growing tree. The tree can then continue being fed by the seed/root to the point of bearing fruit. And the fruit has in it the seed it came out of, which is *also* the seed that is the surety of the (so-called) "future" ongoing life of the tree. This is what we see described in the Genesis 1:11 account of the fruit "whose seed is in itself."

"Knowledge" alone is as the seed, dead and lifeless, and not able to give lasting life. When the seed "falls into the ground and dies" (as did Jesus being buried in the earth), it is resurrected to a new form of itself that we call a tree (which in parallel truth is wisdom; Mary at the tomb did not at first recognize the new wisdom form of the Jesus knowledge). And if the tree "continues in the word" (the nutrition and direction supplied by the word/seed/root), it will bear fruit (understanding), by which it can continue its life forever through the seed in its fruit that can sprout and bear innumerable trees and fruit.

This is key. If you forget everything else in this writing and only recall one thing, remember this: Only true and complete understanding of Truth can enable us to live and not die. As King David said, "Give me understanding, and I shall live" (Psalm 119:144).

Ezekiel 18:31-32 also confirms that a person may avoid death:

"Cast away from you all your transgressions, whereby ye have transgressed; and make you a new heart and a new spirit: for why will ye die, O house of Israel? For I have no pleasure in the death of him that dieth, saith the Lord GOD: wherefore turn yourselves, and **live ye**."

God has no pleasure in the disintegration of your body. We will be discussing why this is so.

Two Important Points

You cannot *force* the transformation in you that is necessary to avoid death. Enoch first obtained "a testimony that he pleased God" (Hebrews 11:5), and this testimony placed him in a position to avoid dropping his physical body in what man calls "death."

So it is important not to think a person can just simply say to himself, "I'm not going to die. I refuse to die" – while thinking it will happen simply by him saying it is so, without first completely understanding what it means and how it happens that he can "please God." One must know what it means to "please" and what the "God" is that he pleases. And you must know exactly how you obtain this testimony (or witness, or report) that you please God. This is discussed further in Chapter 8.

Another important point is that others around you may not know or agree that you have obtained this testimony that Enoch and Jesus received. Why? Because it is *your* experience to experience ... in the same way that no one else can be born for you. It is your birth experience, as you enter the Kingdom of God.

When you finish reading this and meditating upon it and acting upon what you are led of God to do, you will be on your way toward obtaining this testimony.

Why have we believed that we must first be overcome by death, in order to then overcome death?!

CHAPTER 2

If You Wish to be Truly Free, How Can You Argue for Your Own Death?

Man instinctively strives for freedom in his life experience. Jesus said in John 8:32, "The truth shall make you free." Free from what? Everything or anything BUT death? When we are not free, we are in bondage, and Hebrews 2:15 says the work of God is to "deliver them who through *fear of death* were all their lifetime subject to *bondage.*"

The Bible's promise is that we can be FREE. But remember that **partial freedom doesn't exist. Neither does partial health.** One cannot be truly free, for example, if he is made free from sin, but not also free from the paycheck of sin, which is death. (Romans 6:23 says that the wages of sin is death.)

Simply walking out of a jail cell does not make you free, if you are then walking around in a cell with walls that are wider apart, but still present! No walls at all is true freedom.

In John 8:21 and 24, Jesus warns that "ye shall die in your sins." He is pointing out that sinning results in physical death. In verse 35 he states that a servant of "sin" does not abide in the house (meaning, the physical body) forever. But then Jesus said in the next verse, John 8:36, "If the Son (the Son of God, which is Understanding) shall make you free, you shall be free indeed." How can anyone be "free indeed" if he or she has overcome ALL BUT death?!

Revelation 21:7 says that he who overcomes shall "inherit all things." One of these "all" things that can be inherited is "everlasting life," according to Matthew 19:29. **Why have we believed that we must first be *overcome by* death in order to then *overcome death*?! How foolish to say we must be overcome by a thing ... in order to overcome it! How foolish to think the sanctifying work of God in your life transforms your mind, but not your body!**

It is an odd thing that when many people hear this new understanding of the message of the bible, they will resist it – probably because if they were to admit the truth of it, they would have to admit they believed wrong and taught it wrong for years and even decades! Well, SO WHAT? We've all walked the path of espousing error as truth. So get over it! *Get for yourself the benefit* of grasping just how FREEING this message is, that the work of God is not limited in our lives. God does not want to only save your soul – He also wants to save your body!

We are *not* told we can overcome *many or most* of the seeming obstacles in our life. We are not told that death is a sure thing, unavoidable. We are told that "ALL that the Father has is yours!" (Luke 15:31, 1 Corinthians 3:21-23). The Father "has Life in Himself" (John 5:26), and this Life is also ours, since all that the Father has is ours.

Now, I know that for many people who are bible students, there are some verses in the bible that immediately come to mind, verses that supposedly (we've been told) decree in no uncertain terms that *we must each die*. We will address these verses. I hope you will not be one who reads this, only to dismissively refuse the truth of it. *Do not place yourself in the group that is in the rather undesirable position of actually **arguing for their own death!***

The purpose of this book is to guide you to the place where you do not argue for your own death. I used to insist that I needed to die. I've done it. You've done it. We've all done it, but that doesn't mean we should keep on doing it! Arguing for our need to die is an old way of thinking that needs to be forgotten. This book is written so that the old ideas about death will join other erroneous ideas thrown out on the ash pile of forgetfulness -- like for example, thinking that God might actually break a sweat when fighting the devil. Please! What were we thinking?! Even our views about what the "devil" is need to be purged and purified by the fire of Truth.

There are a lot of ways people argue for their own need to die. They refuse to think about the implications of what they say they believe. They ignore the fact that the scriptures say that all things are possible to them that believe that all things are possible. They look around at all the churches that have graveyards just outside the church, and they are willing to continue assuming that churches and dying are an unbreakable association. They decide the price is too high to do the spiritual work of unlearning old ideas, because it is painful sometimes to confront realities that are at odds with the teachings and ideas of their fellow church-goers, their parents, teachers, and friends. They choose to avoid the embarrassment of admitting they believed and taught death acceptance. They may even reject a book that offers the idea of death being overcome before it overcomes the individual.

As my spiritual mentor Dr. Lillie always said, "Don't try to prove me or anyone else wrong. That is the wrong attitude. Prove yourself right."

"In the way of righteousness is life; and in the pathway thereof there is no death."

–Proverbs 12:28

CHAPTER 3

It Is Scriptural, That We Can Conquer Death

The apostle Peter preached that God is not a respecter of persons (Acts 10:34). This means that what is available to one, is available to all. According to the bible, our brothers Enoch, Elijah and Jesus departed from this plane of existence without having to leave their bodies behind to decay. So can you ... IF you choose life instead of death.

Deuteronomy 30:19 says this clearly: "I have set before you life and death, blessing and cursing: therefore choose life, that both thou and thy seed [meaning, your words] **may live**."

The implications of this verse are profound: why are we given a choice to CHOOSE LIFE AND NOT DEATH ... if we truly don't have a choice?! Would the Father dangle such an awesome promise before us, only to make it impossible for humans to experience it?!

Following is a listing of bible verses that show us that we do not need to die. These verses have been in the Old Testament and New Testament scriptures for thousands of years, for those to see who have grown to the place where they can receive the truth of this message. *Are you one that can receive this truth?*

Chapter 3

Many have read and re-read the verses in the bible hundreds and thousands of times in their life. I pray that you will see them now in a new light. Prayerfully and with an open mind read the scriptures quoted and then step back and **ask yourself the questions you read in this chapter, in chapter 5, and elsewhere in this book.**

Remember that the writings and commandments given in the bible are described as having been given to achieve a particular purpose of our Creator. We are told that we should walk with God and be obedient to the leading of God as to how we should live our lives. Why?

Is it because God somehow feels better when we follow His commandments? Does God somehow feel diminished when we don't? No! Over and over and over again we see that the reason, the purpose, the pleasure, the intent of God is that you, personally, will not die, *but live and remain in a body.* Later in this book we will discuss the characteristics of this body.

It's worth taking your time to go through these verses slowly and consider both the individual verses as *well as the collective weight of the Message of Life* in them. Note that the point, or reason God expresses the information in so many, many repetitive ways is, **"that ye may live."** The desire of our Creator is that we would avoid the disintegration of our body. Over and over we see the same concept, that the whole point of God's Word to us is THAT WE WOULD NOT DIE, BUT LIVE ON EARTH IN AN IMMORTALIZED BODILY FORM ONCE OUR MIND HAS BEEN RENEWED.

In the following verses we are focusing on substantiating

the idea that we can avoid death. There are also many traditional religious-sounding words and phrases in the verses that may cause a lot of folks' eyes to glaze over -- words like "righteousness," "sin," "devils," "thee" and "thou." *In various parts of this book and other writings from this author, we will present an understanding of these words.* So for the sake of this chapter discussing the fact that overcoming death is found throughout the bible, we suggest focusing here on the phrases about life, living, death and dying. But as discussed in the preface of this book, make a note of other words and phrases you are unclear about. Ask your Guidance Within for understanding of them, and watch and see how this will come about in you as you seek with a right spirit, and expectancy, and a willingness to look at things differently.

There are so MANY phrases such as "Israel," "Lord," "heaven," "idols" etc that can be, and now *must be understood, rather than parroted, guessed about, pompously preached about, and used as a hammer* to make people feel guilty and unworthy. There are literally millions of websites, books, videos and other resources that purport to give people understanding of bible terms, but evidently thousands of years of these teachings haven't fixed mankind's inability to overcome fear, "sin," and death. So always look within for the True Teacher to speak to you. It's time now for a new, living, lighted understanding of the words we have so casually used without having the foggiest idea of what their true meaning is that will bring victory and overcoming in people's lives.

Remember: parroting dead words (words not understood) will not produce eternal life for you!

So with that said, let us begin with the following verse, because it provides a useful context for seeing the other verses.

Proverbs 12:28
In the way of righteousness is life; and in the pathway thereof there is **no death**.

No death. Zip death. Zero death. Not "just a certain type of death," but NO death.

This is a very powerful verse. It is a key verse for those who have been taught by religious leaders that death of the body is not prevented by the cleansing work of God in our lives, but that "eternal death, burning in hell" is the only kind of death that Jesus came to prevent in making God's righteousness available to mankind. No, there is a path you can walk, in which there is no death at all. This path is called "righteousness," which is the Christ Mind (or Wisdom, or Consciousness) that we are told to walk in. It is described as a clothing, garment, or robe one must "put on." (See Job 29:14, Psalms 132:9, Romans 13:12,14 etc.) It is also called a tree and its fruit, a woman and her offspring, or a Mind and the works that spring forth from it.

Understanding that there is a way we can walk in our journey here on earth that includes NO death, keep this verse in mind as you consider the other verses about death and life presented here. Comments are included in brackets.

Genesis 2:16-17
And the LORD God commanded the man, saying, Of every tree of the garden thou mayest freely eat: But of the tree of the

knowledge of good and evil, **thou shalt not eat of it**: for in the day that thou eatest thereof **thou shalt surely die.** [So by telling man what NOT to do, clearly our Creator's intent was that we wouldn't physically die.]

Genesis 42:2
And he said, Behold, I have heard that there is corn in Egypt: get you down thither, and buy for us from thence; **that we may live, and not die.**

Numbers 4:19
But thus do unto them, **that they may live, and not die,** when they approach unto the most holy things: Aaron and his sons shall go in, and appoint them every one to his service and to his burden.

Deuteronomy 4:1
Now therefore hearken, O Israel, unto the statutes and unto the judgments, which I teach you, for to do them, **that ye may live, and go in and possess the land** which the LORD God of your fathers giveth you. [Deuteronomy has a number of verses showing that the plan of God is that we would live.]

Deuteronomy 5:33
Ye shall walk in all the ways which the LORD your God hath commanded you, **that ye may live,** and that it may be well with you, and **that ye may prolong your days** in the land which ye shall possess.

Deuteronomy 16:20
That which is altogether just shalt thou follow, **that thou mayest live, and inherit the land** which the Lord thy God giveth thee.

Deuteronomy 30:2,6
(When thou) shalt obey his voice…the LORD thy God will circumcise thine heart…to love the LORD thy God with all thine heart, and with all thy soul, **that thou mayest live.**

Psalm 119:17
Deal bountifully with thy servant, **that I may live, and keep thy word.**

Proverbs 14:27
The fear of the LORD is a fountain of life, **to depart from the snares of death. [It just can't get any plainer than this, can it?]**

Amos 5:4, 14
For thus saith the Lord unto the house of Israel, **Seek ye me, and ye shall live**…Seek good, and not evil, **that ye may live**: and so the Lord, the God of hosts, shall be with you, as ye have spoken.

John 6:49-50
Your fathers did eat manna in the wilderness, and are dead. This is the bread which cometh down from heaven, **that a man may eat thereof, and not die.**

John 20:30-31
And many other signs truly did Jesus in the presence of his disciples, which are not written in this book: But **these are written** that ye might believe that Jesus is the Christ, the Son of God; and **that believing ye might have life** through his name.

Ephesians 6:2,3
Honour thy father and mother; (which is the first commandment with promise;) **that it may be well with thee, and thou mayest live long on the earth.**

Hebrews 12:9
Shall we not much rather be in subjection unto the Father of spirits**, and live**?

Psalm 49:20
Man that is in honor, and understandeth not, is like the beasts that perish. [Again, understanding, not just knowledge or wisdom, is necessary to avoid death.]

Psalm 119:144
Give me understanding, and I shall live.

Proverbs 4:20-22
My son, attend to my words…Let them not depart from thine eyes; keep them in the midst of thine heart. **For they are life unto those that find them, and health to all their flesh.** [The implications of the use of the word "all" here are significant. This means health down to the cellular, atomic and

subatomic levels. Life-giving words received by revelation from Wisdom do just that, give life. They quicken every part of the bodily temple.]

Proverbs 10:2
Righteousness delivereth from death. [This is another very succinct verse that parallels what is discussed earlier about Proverbs 12:28.]

Ezekiel 18:31-32
Cast away from you all your transgressions...and make you a new heart and a new spirit. For **why will ye die, O house of Israel? For I have no pleasure in the death of him that dieth** ... therefore turn yourselves, and **live ye.** [These verses in Ezekiel were also presented in Chapter 1, but are also added here, as they bear repeating. The scriptures say that all things are created for His pleasure (Revelation 4:11), and here we see that death is not God's pleasure, or will.]

Matthew 10:8
Heal the sick, cleanse the lepers, **raise the dead,** cast out devils: freely ye have received, freely give...

John 5:24
Verily, verily, I say unto you, He that heareth my word, and believeth on him that sent me, **hath** [NOW, in the present tense] **everlasting life,** and shall not come into condemnation; but **is passed** [NOW, already] from death unto life.

[Clearly the "believing" in this verse occurs NOW, and having the everlasting life is also for NOW.]

John 6:58
This is that bread which came down from heaven: not as your fathers did eat manna, and are dead; he that eateth of this bread shall live forever.

John 8:51
Verily, verily, I say unto you, If a man keep my saying, he shall **never** see death.

John 11:25-26
Jesus said unto her, I am the resurrection, and the life: he that believeth in me, though he were dead, yet shall he live: **And whosoever liveth and believeth in me shall never die. Believest thou this?**
["Never" means not at all, in no way.]

John 10:27-28
My sheep hear my voice, and I know them, and they follow me: And I give unto them eternal life; and they shall **never** perish...

John 14:12
He that believeth on me, the works that I do, shall he do also; and greater works than these shall he do... [Jesus was able to dismiss his spirit and return to his body, and to raise others from the dead, such as Lazarus. The "greater"

works are those done in the fullness of the Father, who Jesus said is "greater than I." The Father is Understanding. Jesus had not yet ascended unto the Father (John 20:17), and told Mary not to cling to him because the Father was Who he said all should focus on. To fall short of the Father / Understanding, was to have faith and hope without charity -- see 1 Corinthians 13.]

Acts 26:8
Why should it be thought a thing incredible with you, that God should raise the dead?

Romans 2:6-7
(God) who will render to every man according to his deeds: To them who…**seek…for immortality**, eternal life. [This is a profound verse written by the apostle Paul, endorsing the seeking of immortality. This corresponds to Paul's admonition in 1 Corinthians that our mortal body must put on immortality. It also ties in to Romans 8:11 shown below.]

Romans 6:23 and 8:2
The wages of sin is death…the law of the Spirit of life in Christ Jesus hath made me **free from** the law of sin and **death.** [If we are free from the law (or governing) of "sin" now, we are also free from death now.]

Romans 8:11-13
If the spirit of him that raised up Jesus from the dead dwell in you, he that raised up Christ from the dead shall also **quicken your mortal bodies** … if ye live after the flesh, ye shall die: but if ye

through the Spirit do mortify the deeds of the body, ye shall live. [Remember that one must be in possession of a mortal body, not having put it off, for a quickening of a "mortal" body to occur.]

2 Corinthians 1:9-10
But we had the sentence of death in ourselves, that we should not trust in ourselves, but in **God which raiseth the dead: Who delivered** us from so great a death, and **doth deliver**: in whom we trust that **he will yet deliver** us. [Note the three tenses -- past, present, and future deliverance from death!]

Hebrews 11:5
By faith Enoch was translated **that he should not see death**; and was not found, because God had translated him: for before his translation he had this testimony, that he pleased God.

2 Peter 3:9
The Lord is ... not willing that any should perish...

1 Corinthians 15:54
So when this corruptible [mind] shall have put on incorruption, and this mortal [body] shall have put on immortality, then shall be brought to pass [in your personal experience] the saying that is written, Death is swallowed up in victory. [Many people have been taught that death being swallowed up in victory occurs as a corporate event to a group of people, all at once, and/or that this victory occurs in a (so-called) future

event in an end-times scenario. But death being swallowed up in victory happens in the experience of an individual, when the work of the Spirit in him or her has been completed. It occurs at the moment the individual "sees (understands) the Father (Life) as He is." See 1 John 3:2.]

1 John 3:6,9
Whosoever abideth in him **sinneth not** ... whosoever is born of God doth not commit sin…and he **cannot sin**, because he is born of God. [Remember that the paycheck, or wages, of sin is death. When one cannot sin, why should he expect to receive the wages of sinning? See chapter 6 in this book on what "sinning" is.]

John 3:16
God so loved the world, that he gave his only begotten Son, that whosoever believeth in him **should not perish, but have everlasting** life. [Remember Proverbs 12:28, that in the way of righteousness is NO death, none, of any kind that someone can try to imagine.]

1 Thessalonians 5:23
I pray God your whole spirit and soul and **body be preserved** blameless unto the coming of our Lord Jesus Christ. [Note that the "coming of the Lord" is the coming to (the awareness of) a person *individually, at whatever period in earth's history that he or she may live.* Why else were so many verses in the New Testament showing that the disciples were even 2000 years ago looking for the appearing of the Lord

Jesus Christ, and advising others to do so? It's because this coming or appearing is an individual thing. It is "to (specifically) those who (personally) look for him," whether living in 200 A.D., 1650 A.D., or 2021. All are to "look for and hasten this appearing" (2 Peter 3:12). It has always been this way, for Enoch, for Elijah, for Jesus, and others. And likewise you are encouraged to look for and hasten the climactic moment when you, like Elijah and Enoch will be caught up, when you will ascend, when you will be able to come and go like the wind.

Are we to believe God raised up Lazarus from the dead to show us that overcoming death and sickness is available for special people, but not for all?

CHAPTER 4

Inconvenient Lazarus

When most folks read the story of Jesus resurrecting Lazarus from the dead, they focus on the fact that Jesus performed a "miracle" that was one more proof that Jesus was sent from God. It's a powerful image to read about this man, Lazarus, coming out of a tomb, still wound with grave cloth, alive after being dead, after responding to the loud voice of Jesus to "come forth."

We also read how the resurrection of Lazarus caused the religious crowd to become even more desirous of destroying Jesus. The bible describes how after being raised from the dead, Lazarus was very much a person of interest. Many people came to see him (John 12:9). Both he and Jesus became the focus of much attention.

So here are some questions to consider. Lazarus had been sick prior to his death. After being raised from the dead, was he still sick, but alive? Was only a certain portion of his body "fixed" by his resurrection, making just enough improvements to bring him into animation and consciousness, but barely making him alive? How did he look? Like a zombie?

For the sake of discussion, let us say he was 30 years old when he died. Did he still look 30 years old after being raised from the dead? Did experiencing death and also the powerful resurrection force of Life make him appear the same, or older, or younger?

How much better off were his kidneys and immune function, after being resurrected, than they were ten years, ten days, or ten minutes prior to dying? How long, in minutes, days or months after his resurrection did his immune cells and the cells in his kidneys and DNA in his body continue robustly alive, before they began to decay? The point of these questions is to ask: Did he begin dying again the first second he walked out of the tomb?

As he looked forward in his life's journey, did he plan on dying again? After being resurrected, did he ever plan on being sick again? If he ever did become sick, would he plan on finding one of the 70 followers Jesus had told to heal the sick? (See Luke 10:9.)

Did Mary and Martha decide that they too would overcome physical death, after seeing what their brother experienced?

Did the daughter of Jairus, who was raised from the dead by Jesus, plan on becoming sick and dying again after having experienced being raised from the dead and **"made whole"**? (Luke 8:50.) Did her parents who saw her be raised plan on dying themselves?

Are we to believe that it's only "one to a customer," for being raised from the dead -- that after Lazarus was raised, he had "used up" his one-per-customer get-out-of-the-tomb-free coupon, so to speak? Are we to believe that the reason God raised up Lazarus and Jairus' daughter, and healed others who hadn't yet died, was to show us that **overcoming death and sickness is available for special people, but not for all?** Are we to believe that the same savior who "abolished death, and hath brought life **and immortality** to light" (2 Timothy 1:10), does not make immortality available while one still has a mortal body?

How are we to view John 5:24 that says, "He that heareth my word, and believeth on him that sent me, HATH everlasting life, and shall not come into condemnation; but IS PASSED FROM death unto life"? If I'm driving on the road and cross a state boundary into the next state, is it not true that I am *now, not later,* "passed from" the last state into the next state?

Doesn't being "passed from death to life" necessarily mean that Life impacts the tissues of my body NOW? Do not forget that the Living Word of Life, when meditated upon, has a biochemical effect on the cells and DNA and organs of your physical body. Your brain is altered. Your bodily hormones are altered. You become more and more a person of Peace, and this has benefit to the entire physical body.

Since the Father does not "have" Life, but IS Life, how far can one go, who is seeking to be "one-with the Father," in terms of merging with and manifesting this Life while still here in a physical body? Exactly where would the dividing line be, for how much Life we can be "one-with"? In other words, how would we say, "you can be one-with God/Life this much, but not THAT much? And which organ system(s) in our bodies does the Word of God, when spoken and meditated on, NOT benefit?

Enoch demonstrated that one can walk so closely with God that at some point he or she will be absorbed up into the higher realms without ever experiencing the death of the physical body!

Life CANNOT die. If it could die, it could obviously not BE Life!

If we are made in His likeness and "shall be like Him" (1 John 3:2), and have been made partakers of His Divine Nature (2 Peter 1:4), **are we not ALSO Life-that-cannot-die** unless we die because we "sign for that package"? **Don't sign for that package!**

Does not being "free from the law of sin and death" as the apostle Paul described, necessarily offer to us the hope of also overcoming the degradation and ending of our physical temple? Could it be that the temple Jesus said he would raise up in three "days" (three lights – knowledge, wisdom, and understanding) is not just his bodily temple, but your bodily temple as well, if you "follow him" as he commanded?

Lazarus knew that he personally had been resurrected by Jesus / the Word of God (the Message of Life). Having had his own experience of being resurrected and walking around, visible, alive on earth again, and knowing that Enoch and Elijah never died – did Lazarus view death to the body as God's plan for people? Did he plan on dying?

Do you?

The work of God (Life) is to swallow up mortality in you. This is what happened to brother Enoch and others.

CHAPTER 5

The Questions We Must Each Answer After Reading the "Life, Not Death" Verses

Here are some of the questions mentioned at the beginning of chapter 3, for your contemplation. The first two are similar, but one addresses death, and one addresses life.

In John 11:26 Jesus says that whoever lives and believes in him shall NEVER die, and John 3:16 says that the one who believes in him should not perish, but *have* EVERLASTING life.

1. **WHEN DOES <u>"NEVER"</u> DYING BEGIN… <u>AFTER</u> YOU DIE?!**

2. **WHEN DOES <u>"EVERLASTING"</u> LIFE BEGIN… <u>AFTER</u> YOU DIE?!**

Everything God does, and everything you will do as you "work the works of God" (John 6:28) is motivated by, soaked in, covered in and results in … Life! This is because "God" IS Life. God does not "have" Life, the way some people think of the term, but the scriptures say that God IS Life.

Proverbs 8:34-36 says: "Blessed is the man that heareth me, watching daily at my gates, waiting at the posts of my doors. For **whoso findeth me findeth Life,** and shall obtain favour of the Lord. But he that sinneth against me wrongeth his own soul: all they that hate me love death."

In John 14:6, Jesus said, "**I am** the way, the truth, and **the Life**."

The work of God in you, as you submit to God's will and are therein "pruned" and disciplined, results in an increase in Life in you -- in your words, in your actions, in your body, and in how you see yourself as one-with God-Who-IS-Life!

It is worth noting that the Bible always brings focus to the central importance of Life. Here are some of the amazing concepts that we read about:

The Word of Life
The Spirit of Life
The Water of Life
The Tree of Life
The Crown of Life
The Prince of Life
The Book of Life
The Path of Life
The Fountain of Life
The Way of Life
The Wellspring of Life
The Bread of Life
The Light of Life
The Newness of Life
The Grace of Life

As you grow in the knowledge of God (not merely knowledge about God, but the knowledge that God IS), Life manifests to a greater and greater degree in you and through you. As you meditate on the words of Life and become more conscious of Life, and as Life flows in an ever-increasing manner through you, *your body biochemically benefits* from this flow of Life. Remember Proverbs 4:20-22, where we read:

"My son, attend to **my words**; incline thine ear unto my sayings. Let them not depart from thine eyes; keep them in the midst of thine heart. For **they are life unto those that find them, and health to all their flesh.**"

If you "endure to the end" (in which you are perfect and entire, lacking nothing), you will **be** saved -- spirit, soul and body. See Matthew 24:13, James 1:4, and 1 Thessalonians 5:23. It is also useful to look up the large number of bible verses that contain the word "endure."

It is very clear in the scriptures that Life has a work that it is doing in your mind and in your physical temple, or body. This work is very clearly stated in 2 Corinthians 5:4:

"For we that are in this tabernacle do groan, being burdened: not for that we would be unclothed, but clothed upon, **that mortality might be swallowed up of life**."

The work of God (Life) is to swallow up mortality in you. This is what happened to brother Enoch and others.

This brings us to yet another question you must answer.

3. DO YOU CHOOSE TO EXPERIENCE MORTALITY BEING SWALLOWED UP IN YOU?

Is this your desire, that Life would so flow through you that you do as Jesus did, and one day simply become invisible as you vibrate at the frequency of Life and ascend into the higher realms?

Do you desire that every atom, molecule, tissue and organ in your physical body would express Life in its fullness? To do so requires a process of what the Bible calls "forsaking." We must forsake our illusions that are brought about by being governed by "sin." In our next chapter we will speak about what it means to no longer be ruled by sin.

All truth is parallel. Remember that you are what you eat. When you ingest Life, when you consume-it-by-meditation-on-it, you become Life. So make a decision that you will eat the Bread of Life and become everything that it enables you to be and remember. We must all consciously become as our Father/Source is.

As you meditate on Divine ideas, you will partake of the Divine Nature. It occurs as you think, speak, and act on the leading of God. That we are to ingest Divine truth, to bring it IN to your heart and to meditate on it, is described in Deuteronomy 6:6-7:

"These words, which I command thee this day, shall be

in thine heart: And thou shalt teach them diligently unto thy children, and shalt talk of them when thou sittest in thine house, and when thou walkest by the way, and when thou liest down, and when thou risest up."

How can the Spirit "quicken your mortal body" (Romans 8:11) if you no longer have a mortal body to be quickened?

CHAPTER 6

About "Sinning" and Being "Appointed Once to Die"

Preachers and teachers have indoctrinated people for generations that there is no choice but to die, since (they say) the bible tells us that every person is "appointed unto death." They quote the book of Hebrews in support of this erroneous idea.

Hebrews 9:26-28 says, "Now *once* in the end of the world hath he appeared to *put away sin* by the sacrifice of himself. And as **it is appointed unto men ONCE to die,** but after this the judgment: So Christ was *once* offered to bear the sins of many…"

The death or dying each man is appointed to is not physical, bodily death, but as Romans 6:9-12 says, it is **dying to "sin,"** which means *dying to living by the dictates of your senses.* When the senses no longer govern you, but you rule them and have proven to yourself that you rule them, **then** you *"cannot sin."* Then will come to pass *in you* the words of Matthew 1:21: "Jesus (the Word/Will of God, lived out by you)…shall save his people from their sins."

Let us read Romans 6:9-11: "Knowing that Christ being raised from the dead dieth no more … **For in that he died, he died unto sin ONCE … Likewise reckon ye also yourselves** to be dead indeed unto sin, but alive unto God through Jesus Christ our Lord…"

Every person *does* need to *die once … to sin*. The verse says that "likewise" we are to be dead to sin.

Don't let this slip by you without grasping it: "sin," has not been understood, in terms of what God says sin is. **Sin, or "sinning" IS living by and being governed by the dictates of your senses.** When one is ruled by his or her senses, he or she then does the actions that result from being governed in this manner. "Sinning," since the senses provide incomplete and incorrect information as to how one should live his life, results in disintegration of the human body, what man calls "death." In Hebrews 3:17 we read that sinning caused the people journeying toward the promised land to experience having their carcasses (bodies) fall in the wilderness. The children of Israel wandered through the "Wilderness of Sin" (Exodus 16:1).

Isaiah 11:3 gives us the pattern by which we are to live our lives, relative to our senses of seeing, hearing, etc. We read: "he shall not judge after the sight of his eyes, neither reprove after the hearing of his ears." *It's not that we are to ignore or not use our senses, but that our judgments not be **ruled by** our senses.*

Actions such as harming others and indulging in unbalanced practices and addictions will over time disappear as one more and more lives in the "place" where he or she is no longer governed by what the senses say (such as when our senses tell us that this or that looks good, sounds good, feels good, is pleasurable, etc). A dead person can no longer react or be moved, no matter how strenuously someone attempts to stimulate the sensory organs by yelling in the dead person's ear or poking his body.

No longer being governed by the senses has a tremendous number of benefits. In addition to helping preserve our bodies, not being governed by the senses helps one avoid the great deception that is so strong that if it were possible, it could deceive the elect ones (Matthew 24:24). That deception occurs when people are deceived by outer understandings reached by sensory inputs. I cannot overemphasize how important "getting this" is, now, today, as sensory inputs guiding and governing our actions and reactions have and will have significant consequences. Many things will "look like" they make "sense," as explained by leaders and groups, but they are a lie. Our senses, of themselves, can only "know in part."

We see in the 3rd chapter of James that there are two kinds of wisdom [mind], and that man's earthly wisdom is "*sensual*" (derived from the senses). The incomplete information provided to our mind by our senses can deceive and enslave us. The fruit Eve ate and gave to Adam came from the tree that Eve "*saw…that it was pleasant to the eyes*" (Genesis 3:6). Eve's sense of sight *overruled* what she knew God had told her.

"Sin" is not something you do, but rather something that "reigns over," or has "dominion over" you.

Romans 6:12, 14, 16-18 are very useful here; see how many times the apostle Paul speaks of sin ruling over a person who obeys the sin:

"Let not sin therefore **reign** in your mortal body, **that ye should obey it** in the lusts thereof…for sin shall not have **dominion over** you…Know ye not, that to whom ye yield yourselves servants to obey, **his servants ye are to whom ye obey**; whether of sin unto death, or of obedience unto righteousness? But God be thanked, that ye were the **servants of sin**, but ye have obeyed from the heart that form of doctrine which was delivered you. **Being then made free from sin, ye became the servants of righteousness."**

The thing(s) you do while "sinning" (being governed by the dictates of your senses) is not what we should exclusively focus on, but rather WHAT is *leading you to do* the thing! This is why the apostle Paul spoke of one person being free to do a thing, while another person is not free to do it. It's not the thing itself that is the issue, but who or what is moving you while you are doing it! Romans 14:22-23 says, "Happy is he that *condemneth not himself* in that thing which he *alloweth…* for whatsoever is not of faith is sin."

Now let me insert a very important thing to note here: I am NOT saying that people are free to do horrible things as long as they think they have the freedom to do the things. No! We must still abide by the law of doing unto others as we would have them do unto us. But I am saying that understanding what sin actually IS, can help one to overcome "sin" and "sinning," and thereby avoid death. It is a scriptural thing that while here on earth ONE CAN OVERCOME SIN, and reap the benefits of this overcoming.

Mankind has been told for centuries that only after one physically dies as a result of sin, can a person live. We've been told that the death of Jesus allows one's sins to be washed away … but we must understand that Jesus' death frees us from sin and death **if each of us individually follow his example and**

do as he did -- take up *your own* cross and die to obeying the dictates of your senses. The death of "Jesus" IS important, but we must know what this "Jesus" is that dies! Jesus is the Word/Seed of Knowledge that must die and be raised in a different form (the Tree of Wisdom), and this Tree/Wisdom must go on to bear the fruit of Understanding.

In Hebrews 11:5-6 we read the following concerning Enoch: "By faith [Understanding] Enoch was translated that he should not see death; and was not found, because God had translated him: for before his translation he had this testimony, that he pleased God. But without faith [Understanding] it is impossible to please [be like, or in agreement with] him…"

When you "please" or are in-agreement-with or "like" God and cannot sin, you certainly do not earn the wages or paycheck of sin, which is death!

Why do we think that living under the dictates of sin is something we cannot escape? There are numerous verses describing **life after no longer "sinning."**

1 John 3:6,9 says, "Whosoever abideth in him sinneth not ... Whosoever is born of God *doth not commit sin;* for his seed remaineth in him: and *he cannot sin*, because he is born of God."

1 Peter 4:1-2 speaks about one having the same Christ Mind and "ceasing from sin" and then **after this ceasing,** "living the rest of his time in the flesh to the will of God."

When Jesus refused to condemn the woman caught in adultery in John 8:11, he told her to "Go, and sin no more." Surely he wasn't saying, "Go, and don't do this adultery sin any more, but it's understandable and okay to do other sins."

Chapter 6

1 Corinthians 15 speaks about overcoming sin and death. In verse 34, the Spirit through the apostle Paul says we are to "awake to righteousness, and sin not" (meaning, while here on earth). And verses 53-58 speak about death being swallowed up in victory "when this corruptible shall have put on incorruption, and this mortal shall have put on immortality."

I am going to show you a mystery here. The "corruptible" that must put on incorruption is the corruptible MIND spoken of by the apostle Paul in 2 Corinthians 11:3, 1 Timothy 6:5, and 2 Timothy 3:8, and also referred to as the carnal mind in Romans 8:6-7. The "mortal" that must put on immortality is your mortal body that is "quickened" (made alive) as described by Paul in Romans 8:11.

Romans 8:6 tells us that "to be carnally [sensory] MINDED **is** death," and that "to be spiritually minded **is** life and peace." <u>Fixing the death in the mind allows fixing the death manifesting in the body.</u>

For those who believe the scriptures, but argue against the idea of avoiding death, I would ask this question: How exactly can a person experience the "mortal putting on immortality," as described in 1 Corinthians 15, **if he has died and no longer has a mortal body?!** How can the Spirit "quicken *your* mortal body" as described in Romans 8:11 **if you no longer have a mortal body to be quickened?!**

Millions of people have never, ever thought about the absurdity of saying, "I want to live forever … but first I still need to die!"

Does this mean that no person will lay down their body who "chooses Life" and has reached the place of

Understanding? No, some who choose Life WILL lay down their body because that is the Divine plan for the individual. But they will know that their life is not being "taken" from them. Having obtained Understanding, they are aware of co-creating and being led of God to be in the set of circumstances they find themselves in. Some who lay down their body will have already gone through the ascension process in another incarnation. (Yes, so-called "reincarnation" is biblical and is a real thing, but it does not occur in the way that most have been taught, and you were never a monkey. This subject will be addressed in other writings.) Some may lay their body down and not pick it back up, and others will lay it down and then manifest again in a resurrected form of it. See what Jesus said in John 10:17-18:

"Therefore doth my Father love me, because I lay down my life, that I might take it again. *No man taketh it from me, but I lay it down of myself. I have power to lay it down, and I have power to take it again.* This commandment have I received of my Father."

Note what Jesus said about re-infusing Life into his body. He knew what he had heard from his Father about re-entering his body that he would lay down ... so he did just that! The "power" (Wisdom, or Consciousness) he had to lay down his life and to pick it back is key. *This book is to set you on your own path toward having this power (Consciousness) in you.* It is the Mind Jesus operated in, the one Paul said we are to "let" be in us (Philippians 2:5-6).

Remember that nothing Jesus did and demonstrated for us was to "show off" his power, but rather to show us *what we can do for ourselves* WHEN we are one-with our Father (John 17:21-23) and speak what we hear the Father say (John 12:49-50), and do what we see the Father do (John 5:19).

Jesus did not give up in his desire to fulfill the Father's will. For us also, to choose Life is an ongoing commitment. It is essential to endure to the end, to "faint not" as you journey toward your goal of your "whole body being full of light" (Matthew 6:22).

If this Message bears witness in you, do not give up, as did the folks who walked away from it because they faced trials, loved worldly riches, or because of the "hard sayings" you will encounter (John 6:47-69). Elijah faced numerous trials, but he showed us that WE CAN OVERCOME DEATH.

Yes, "Jesus" (the Word) IS the savior to save us from our sins … but not because he did the dying for you (instead of you), but rather in that he showed you what you must do for yourself. I know this is shocking for many people to hear, but see it this way: Jesus/the Word/the Will of God/knowledge IS the savior in the same way that a seed is the savior enabling a tree to save (continue) its life IF the seed will fall into the ground and die and be resurrected in a new form (a tree/wisdom) that can bear fruit with seed (understanding) in the fruit. *This is why we must "continue in (keep growing in) the Word" and we must "go on to perfection" (to the fruit-bearing/understanding state).*

Jesus did not "do it all" for you! If that was the case, why are we to "work out your own salvation with fear and trembling" (Philippians 2:12) and to "endure temptation" in order to "receive the crown of life" (James 1:12)? If the

holiness of Jesus is all one needs to rely on, why do we read in Hebrews 12:4-11 that must we endure correction and chastening to partake of the Father's holiness? Why all the emphasis on personal "overcoming" in Revelations 2 and 3 as a qualification to be clothed in white, eat from the Tree of Life, etc?

That Jesus did not do everything for you is shown in Hebrews 4:8, which says, "For if Jesus had given them rest, he would not afterward have spoken of another day." The Jesus level of faith is the starting point, a wonderful and *essential foundation* from which to begin as you are "guided into ALL truth" (John 16:13). You must continue in the nutrition and guidance of the "way" (direction of growth that is Jesus/knowledge) until you "get wisdom" (that descends from above) and then finally attain "the Knowledge of the Holy, which is Understanding" (Proverbs 9:10). These three stages of growth are also known as the three baptisms: the baptism of John, the baptism of the Holy Spirit, and the baptism in the Fire.

Ceasing from sin is vital. But it does not happen without undergoing a growth process that includes forsaking old ideas, incorporating new ones, and being a doer of the leading available directly to the individual from the Spirit of God within. We must learn obedience to the Spirit's Voice within that oftentimes is at odds with what our senses would tell us.

You CAN get to the place in your journey here on earth where you do not sin, where you do not live your life governed by the dictates of your senses. There are those that teach their students that "you'll always have some sin in your life. You can't get past it. You ARE a sinner and you WILL be sinning!" But why then would John say in 1 John 2:1, "My little children, these things write I unto you, *that ye sin not*"? Why would he say in 1 John 5:18, "whosoever is born of God sinneth not"? It's because we must come to the place of not "sinning"! We all have sinned … BUT you can reach the point where you no longer sin.

At the end of this chapter I am going to leave you with a powerful confirmation of the fact that we must not let our senses govern us. Consider first a dog that you have known, and imagine it sitting next to you. This dog hears sounds going into your ears that you cannot hear.

Now think of frog swimming in a pond near you. Some frogs are said to see infrared light that does not register in the eyes we humans have.

So here is the key question: **If a dog and a frog have a better picture of reality than you do, using their sensing tools, why would you rely on your limited senses to tell you what is true or false, or how to live your life?** Do you see the cosmic radiation coming from light years away that just passed through your body? Do you hear the sounds that occur before earthquakes? Clearly if you rely on the incomplete information provided by your senses, you will act in ignorance and reach wrong conclusions about yourself, life, death, and God!

We must instead lean on the intuitive knowing we all have inside us that is true Intelligence and Consciousness. Its guidance is always life-ward, tending toward life. Our senses are to support, not rule over this Inner Voice of the True Self.

To "sin" or "live in sin" is to be governed by the dictates of our senses. Our senses may tell us, "eat this, it tastes so good," when in fact that tasty food may harmfully affect our blood chemistry and the health of our body. **If we sin not, we will die not.**

So remember the lesson of the dog and the frog when you make your decisions in your journey here on earth. You will live and not die as you follow this Voice of the Self within that "needs no light from the moon or the sun" (the knowledge and wisdom of man).

John 3:16 (For God so loved the world…) is one of the most quoted bible verses throughout the world. Here is the correct interpretation of it.

CHAPTER 7

The Formless God, and Saving Your House

The point of you being here on earth is to grow in the knowledge of God to the place where your mind is renewed, the words proceeding from this mind through your mouth are quickened, and your body is saved, and you will become a lasting temple of God.

The scriptures call your body by various names, such as "house," and "temple." The intent of the Father is that our mind (body of knowledge) be made incorruptible, and our physical body/house/temple be filled with light and made immortal. **Your mind and body are to be "an habitation of God" (Ephesians 2:22).** *The new mind and body is described in the book of Revelation as a "new heaven and a new earth."*

Our bodies ARE the temple of God. To see a picture of how we are to view the bodies/temples we have, we can read the biblical account of the building of Solomon's temple. Solomon's temple used only the finest materials and talent in its construction.

In the ongoing use of this temple, exactly how much temple structure damage and disrepair do you believe God finds acceptable? And what does God want brought into the temple? Did not Jesus/the Word of God forcefully dislodge and throw out of the temple the things that have no business being in the temple? See Mark 11:15-18. This is what the Word of God does, it cleanses our temples!

In 1 Kings 9:3, do we not see that the house of God was designed to be a place where the God's name would be there ***forever, without interruption?*** Here is the verse:

"And the Lord said unto him, I have heard thy prayer and thy supplication, that thou hast made before me: I have hallowed this house, which thou hast built, to put my name there *for ever*; and mine eyes and mine heart shall be there *perpetually*."

Also see the following verses:

John 8:35 -- The servant abideth not in **the house** for ever: but the Son abideth ever.

Romans 8:23 -- Even we ourselves groan within ourselves, waiting for the adoption, to wit, **the redemption of our body.**

Philippians 3:21 -- (The Lord Jesus Christ) who shall change our vile body, that it may be fashioned like unto his glorious body…

2 Corinthians 4:10,11 -- Always bearing about in the body the dying of the Lord Jesus, **that the life also of Jesus might be made manifest in our body.** For we which live are always delivered unto death for Jesus' sake, that the life also of Jesus might be **made manifest in our mortal flesh**.

The Father desires to bring your mind and body to the place of perfection and everlasting life. For you, this may have required incarnating in a large number of bodies (incarnations). The point of incarnating is to develop and grow your senses and for you to master them. The goal is that the repetitive wheel of reincarnation for you will end, at which time your body will be immortalized.

The final incarnation is what the bible calls the last "generation" (of a body – see Matthew 24:34). This generation shall not pass away (die) until all things be fulfilled in you.

When all of the sanctifying work of God is done in your mind and body, then the "fire" will come down and the "glory" of the Lord will fill your house. This is seen in the story in 2 Chronicles, chapters 5, 6, and 7 about the dedication of the temple Solomon built.

In 2 Chronicles 7:1 we read: "When Solomon had made an end of praying, the fire came down from heaven, and consumed the burnt offering and the sacrifices; and the glory of the LORD **filled the house**."

Do you wish for the Fire/Understanding of the Holy One to 100% fill and preserve you and your house/body? IF you can believe it and forsake all your old, preconceived ideas about who and what you are, you can receive it!

Who are you? "You" live and move and have your being **in** God, and "**in** him is NO darkness at all!" [See Acts 17:28 and 1 John 1:5.] You – the real you, not the imagined you – are Light! *What else could you be, since you exist IN God Who IS Light?!*

We have overlooked this message for thousands of years, though it was right in front of us.

Jesus said, "Man shall not *live by* bread alone, but by every word that proceeds out of the mouth of God." Paul said that, "The just shall *live by* faith." The point Jesus and Paul were clearly making is: **to live!**

It is obvious when you finally "see it," that the message told over and over again throughout the Bible is that LIFE in its FULLNESS is possible, when one pays the price to forsake the senses-derived lies he or she has believed about Reality. The senses only provide partial knowledge of Reality, and most of that information is incorrect. **"Knowing in part must be done away" (1 Corinthians 13:9-13).**

Believe as the majority of people have, and you will die. Jesus did not come to teach us how to die. But if you want to LIVE and see the victory over death that Jesus and others spoke of, make ONE decision: that you will seek Truth at the cost of all else … and then make every other decision in support of that one key decision.

"God" is a formless God that changes not. It/God is what we have termed "everywhere" (but the term "where" is not real), and being everywhere, God abides or resides in Itself. Nothing else "outside" of Itself exists or could ever exist for It to abide "in." It/God so loved (so desired) the experience of Itself in a form (body), that It created us as a seed that could awaken and grow to know itself/the seed forever as the formless One IN the seed. This is the true understanding and interpretation of the well-known verse John 3:16!

We must first awaken to know What we live in. Then we grow to find out that since we abide or live in It, It *must be* IN us, and therefore IS us! And we are It! Then will come to pass Jesus' words in John 14:23: "If a man love me [love the Truth], he will keep my words: and my Father will love him, and we will *come unto* him, and make our abode with him" [meaning, within him, the form.] This "coming unto" the person is the glory of the Lord [the Understanding of Self] that comes to (is remembered by) the temple/form, as we can read in the parable/parallel story of the glory of the Lord filling the temple when Solomon dedicated the temple he built.

We build the temple of God, the form of the formless One, by speaking words that have been quickened/made alive by the Spirit of Truth within us. The words are the result of meditating on Living (revealed/alive) Truth, and these living words quite *naturally* come out of our heart and through our mouth. So a living, resurrected **body of knowledge** in us expresses living words that give life to both our physical body and to the minds and bodies of those who hear us! We can then say, "MY words, they are Spirit and they are Life," as did Jesus. We realize that "I" AM my words, and my words ARE "I-as-them." God is Its Word ("the Word WAS God") and I am likewise in, through, and as my words.

The "Son of God" that gives us eternal life is a body of knowledge that is birthed out of heavenly Wisdom. This Son of God is Understanding, which is called the "Knowledge of the Holy" in the bible (Proverbs 9:10). The Son of Man that we read about in the bible must be sacrificed. This level of awareness must be done away with in order for us to obtain the Son of God, which is another way of describing the Understanding (fruit) of the Wisdom from Above. The "bondwoman and her son" (the wisdom and understanding of man) must be "cast out" of our house (Galatians 4:30) so that the "free woman and her son" (the Wisdom from Above and the Understanding of the Holy that is her Son) can be our portion. We cannot eternally "save our house" (mind and body) until or unless we create or build a living body by expressing living words of Understanding.

Why are you here on earth in a body? It is so that the Formless One can experience within Itself the experience of you/the form waking up to know yourself as Itself -- and thereby immortalize the form/your body.

Why does God not die? If you do not know the answer, you cannot know what it will take for you to not die also.

CHAPTER 8

Obtaining a Testimony that You Please God

In Hebrews 11:5-6 we read that Enoch did not die, as he "had this testimony, that he *pleased* God." We read that "without faith it is impossible to *please* him," and that "he that *cometh to* God" must believe that he is, and that he is a rewarder of them that diligently seek Him."

To "please" means to agree with; to run parallel with; to be chosen as agreeable. "God" is Truth, or one could say, Reality. So to "please God" MEANS to agree with that which is true and real. The phrase that "without faith it is impossible to please God" MEANS without Understanding, it is impossible to be in agreement with Reality, or Truth.

The scripture advises us to "come to" God. But how can a person "come to" God, since God is everywhere-present? It is impossible to go somewhere that God is not, so clearly coming "to" God is a coming to the awareness of God AS ALL, including being AS me. This knowledge, *when truly realized*, changes the mind and body of the individual in whom this realization occurs. The changes begin on the inside … in your atoms of your DNA, in the arrangements of neurons in your brain, and in your blood chemistry.

On this journey, the seeker will come to know that God can usefully be described or identified as ***Cause***. After he or she has "grown in the knowledge of God" (the Knowledge that IS God), the individual realizes that he himself, being one-with and living inside of God, is Cause-as-himself. He has a revelation about this. It is ALIVE to him. Forsaking one lie about reality after another, choosing to live in the Realm of Cause (the Kingdom of God) rather than accept and live in the illusory world of *effect,* he grows in consciousness until he knows that he "pleases" or is in agreement with Cause. He ceases to believe there are other powers at work anywhere, but knows that there exists only ONE power that is the One Cause. Romans 13:1 tells us that "there is no power but of God."

Why does God (Cause) not cease to exist, or die? If you do not know the answer, you cannot know what it will take for you to not die also.

Here is the answer: "God" (Cause) IS Life.

Life **can't** die.

Cause **must** be (exist).

Effect **can** exist, but **must not** exist. It only exists because Cause IS its existence.

For you to live and not die, you must know WHO you truly are. When you have realized Who and What you are (not just having information about it, or revelation about it, but *realization*), then you know that you ARE Life and **cannot** die! Your body's cells, atoms, genetics and every so-called "part" of you line-up-with and *fully* express this Life that you ARE! This realization occurs at the appointed time; it occurs completely, enveloping every aspect of you; and there is zero doubt in the mind of the person who has *realized* that he IS LIFE!

The Son is like his Father. At the baptism by John, Jesus heard a "voice from heaven which said, Thou art my beloved Son; in thee I am *well pleased.*" Here we see another instance of "having a testimony that you please God [are like/one-with/in agreement with Truth/Reality]."

In Colossians 1:10 we read, "that ye might walk worthy of the Lord unto *all pleasing*, being fruitful in every good work, and increasing in the knowledge of God." And 1 Thessalonians 2:4 says, "we speak, not as pleasing men, but *[pleasing]* God."

During the "transfiguration" described in Matthew 17, a voice came from the bright cloud that overshadowed the group on the mountain, saying, "This is my beloved Son, in whom I am *well pleased*; hear ye him."

Adam's son Abel, who was killed by his brother Cain, similarly had "obtained witness that he was righteous" (Hebrews 11:4). Later in the same chapter we read in verse 39 that those referenced in the chapter had "obtained a good report."

We must all first obtain this testimony, or report, if we are to qualify to be eligible to not die. For some (such as Stephen, in the book of Acts), it is their Divine plan to lay down their body. But it is time now for mankind to wake up to the destiny of many who will move on to the next realm without going through physical dissolution of the body. These are those who will have their body raised to a higher frequency by the renewing of their mind, and then take their transformed body with them as they move into the higher realms of consciousness.

This experience cannot be somehow *forced or made* to happen. It happens when one has grown in the knowledge of God, and has "**laid aside** every weight, and **the sin** which doth so easily beset us" (Hebrews 12:1). It happens when we become one with our Source. This Source, we are told, "is a consuming Fire."

We cannot be born into the Kingdom of God without first going through the process of being trans-formed. It is *a process*. One is not born on earth without first going through stages in the womb of his or her mother. The child starts as a fertilized seed, then becomes an embryo, then a fetus, and finally a baby that can be born into the world.

Many people go to a church service and make a decision to seek after God, and after the prayer the person prays, the ministers have for centuries proclaimed the person is "born again." No, they are not yet born. They are "begotten" (or sired), but they must then go through a growth and development process before the birth occurs, as does any baby in the womb. They are not born again yet. But they have the opportunity to "become" a Son of God (John 1:12), if they will "endure to the end" of their experience in form (Matthew 24:3,13).

Consider the Hard Boiled Egg

Jesus tells us not to judge by the outer appearance (John 7:24). Consider two eggs. One comes directly from a chicken, and the other has been hard boiled in water. Heat makes the difference. They *look* the same from the outside. They both look like eggs. But there is a change that has taken place internally in the hard boiled one due to the heat (fire) it has experienced.

We must all go through the fire of God to be purified. But we must not use our senses to look at ourselves or someone else and make a judgment as to where we or others have arrived in the journey of forsaking illusion.

So don't make foolish statements or reach foolish conclusions as to how far along in the process toward new birth you or someone else has attained. *The work of God in us in an inner work. It is a heart thing. God looks at our heart.* We have all made unwise decisions, but consider how much God loved King David, despite some of David's unwise and harmful decisions.

David wanted to build a "temple" for God, and his psalm said that his one desire was to dwell in the "house" of the "Lord" all the days of his life. He was not allowed to build the temple, but God said to him, "Forasmuch as it was in thine heart to build an house for my name, thou didst well in that it was in thine heart" (2 Chronicles 6:8).

Along with Enoch and Jesus, Elijah is another of the heroes in the bible who never died. In 1 Kings 18:36-38 we read that by the witness of the "fire" Elijah was confirmed by God "that I am thy servant, and that I have done ALL these things at thy word." In other words, he obtained a testimony that he pleased God. **Bear in mind that the story of Elijah and the calling down of the fire is a picture of an inner work that transpired inside Elijah.** The fire of the Lord that fell consumed forever the old, sensory-based knowledge. And after the fire fell, Elijah destroyed the false prophets (words/ideas) that opposed him.

Elijah knew that he would be taken up into heaven without dying (see 2 Kings 2:1,10). He had been willing to die, saying he was no better than his previous incarnations (his "fathers" – see 1 Kings 19:4). But it was in the plan of God for him to ascend by a "whirlwind." This of course is the wind of the Spirit (the Consciousness) that Jesus said would cause those who were born of the Spirit to "come and go" – see John 3:8.

Enoch, Elijah, and Jesus all obtained a testimony that they were living their experience in agreement with God/Truth. They became one-with their Father/Source. They no longer believed in an "other" (their eye was single, not evil, which is to see and believe in something other than the One.) Therefore the Fire that is the Father "consumed" them, absorbing them and trans-forming their temples/bodies, causing them to ascend and live in the "new heaven and new earth" (mind and body) that John described in the book of Revelation.

Is it your desire also to construct a place of residence for the Father to dwell in eternally? This book is written to encourage people to do just that ... and to do it as the Father wishes it to be done, not the way we with our limited senses believe it is to be done.

We believe God has raised the dead who were no longer in their mortal bodies. Surely we must believe God can quicken my mortal body while I'm still in it!

CHAPTER 9

About Your "Ascension" and Your New Body

There are a growing number of people today who speak of humans going through a process of "ascension." This is a useful term to use, but it must be understood in the context of the growth process that occurs during a person's ascension.

The growth process involves changing how you view, well, basically … everything. The culmination of your ascension does not occur without a period of both visible and invisible-to-others changes in your view of self, God, and everything in the universe. Ideas of organized religion will be left behind. Priorities for how you spend your time will shift dramatically. How you eat, who you hang out with, where you live, what you do with your resources, how you view man's governmental systems, all these things may undergo big changes. Your views about science, history, and beings from other realms will be examined by you. You will reach conclusions that startle you. Some of your new understandings will create in you a feeling of deep awe. You will want to know why you showed up here on earth with the body you have and the circumstances into which you were born. Your views about how to discern truth from error will evolve. You will see the extreme value of being wise (having wisdom), rather than simply having information (knowledge).

You will experience changes in your body as you process and incorporate new ideas. You will learn to crave periods of silence, during which time you become familiar with how you may access the true Intelligence within you.

Jesus called this growth process one of "forsaking." The good news is, **the only things we are ever asked to forsake are our illusions of Reality.** One never need forsake That Which is Real.

You will also find that certain people who *profess* that they wish to build an eternal home in their body and consciousness for the Divine One, are not necessarily on this path simply because they say they are. For some, the mental and emotional costs of the forsaking, and the rather humbling things one must face about himself are simply too high of a cost. For others, fatigue can set in, as the growth process can take longer than they would like.

The process is called by some "the quickening." This is also a useful term, as long as one knows what it means. To *quicken* means to *make alive*. Romans 8:11 speaks of your mortal body being quickened.

The quickening is the opposite of the aging process. As the quickening proceeds, one's attitudes become more youthful. Peace, optimism, and willingness to explore are the youthful qualities you will see growing in you as you ascend higher and higher in consciousness. I call it "youthalizing." You become more youthful in your countenance, and a bounce and vigor begin to show up in your step.

You will be led to make lifestyle changes that assist your body, in your diet and how you take care of your bodily temple. You will become a vegetarian if you are not one already. Your new diet and lifestyle may help you improve certain disease states you have experienced. Some folks may experience dramatic disappearances of diseases. For many, though, the complete and ultimate elimination of physical aging, pain, and disease happens in the final climactic culmination of your growth when you are swallowed up by the Fire of God. This "chariot of Fire" took Elijah into the upper realms without him needing to leave behind a decaying, lifeless body.

What kind of a body does Elijah experience and utilize today? What will your body be like, after it is "baptized in the Fire"? Your mind being filled with Understanding, you will experience or acknowledge no limitation, so your body will be one that can shape shift. You will be as your Father is. The body of God shape shifts, for example today it might exist in the form of 9,887 galaxies in one area of the universe, and tomorrow in the form of 9,888 as a new galaxy is formed. You, "like Him" (1 John 3:2), will similarly experience yourself in a vehicle/body that can shape shift (form shift).

It will be a body that can "come and go like the wind" (John 3:8) in various levels and planes of existence. It will always be "you," because you are not separate from your body. "It" is you-as-it.

Your body will not be limited by the ideas of time, distance, and movement. It will always dwell in a state of *now, here, and stillness (movement without movement)*. It will be recognizable as *your* body. It will be genderless, as it will experience no separation or division. It will not die or decay, will not be subject to *needing* outer nutrition coming into it (what we call eating), and it will contain a fully accessible record of all you have ever experienced. It will demonstrate Life in a way that few today can imagine. *It will be the Formless One, in form.*

Is it difficult for you or a loved one to believe that God can quicken people's bodies today, along the lines of what happened to Enoch, Elijah, and Jesus?

Since we believe God has quickened and raised the dead who were no longer in their mortal bodies (Lazarus, etc), surely we must believe He can quicken my mortal body while I'm still in it! He said (in Romans 2:7) to seek immortality!

2 Corinthians 1:9 says that "we should not trust in ourselves, but in God which raiseth the dead." This means that there is no "type" of death (as some would try to differentiate) that cannot be overcome, if one is willing to forsake old ways of thinking and living, and be a doer of the leading of God in his or her life.

Remember that, as the apostle Paul said, "to be carnally minded IS death" (Romans 8:6). To be carnally minded is to be sensory-minded, and living by the dictates of the senses provides only temporary peace and enjoyment (Hebrews 11:25). As you become "spiritually minded" (conscious of being Consciousness), lasting peace will be the hallmark of your experience, and this peace will preserve your body, enhance your enjoyments, and impart to others a lifting of their own state of consciousness. Your presence around others will affect them, by the words you say, the things you do, the Knowledge you possess and demonstrate, and the invisible frequency of Light that you transmit. Seeing no walls in your experience, you will be aware that all things are possible for you.

Religious groups have a history of encouraging parroting of doctrines and discouraging people from thinking independently.

CHAPTER 10

Avoiding Death, for the UnBibled

For the many people who are not familiar with the bible, it is important to know that one does not need to be strongly versed in the bible in order to grow in consciousness to where it is possible to skip death. After all, God is a fair God, and billions of people have never had the benefit of living when or where there was a bible to be read.

But as with bible-oriented people, the first step for those who are "unbibled" is to reorient one's thinking. It is vital to lose the need for the approval of anyone other than the intuitive guiding Voice that is available inside all of us. Most people consciously or unconsciously seek the approval of man, but in no longer seeking that approval, you will become comfortable with the fact that man's religious training is not a prerequisite for spiritual growth. In fact, religious training can be, and frequently is, an obstacle in achieving spiritual understanding and overcoming death.

Religious groups have a history of encouraging parroting of doctrines and discouraging people from thinking independently about a broad spectrum of subjects. But independent, personal examination of issues is essential; otherwise we are relying on second-hand evidence from someone outside ourselves about how to live our lives. First-hand, personal witness to truth can carry us through challenging times. Second-hand truth does not build for the individual a firm foundation that can withstand the storms of life.

Religious groups also often focus on outer works, rather than emphasizing that the primary work of spiritual growth is an inward, mental growth in consciousness. In many religious organizations, there is a lot of emphasis on feeding the hungry, helping the homeless, or observing outer rituals such as lighting candles or putting oil on people's heads or immersing people in pools of water. Of course, helping the less fortunate, as you are led of God to do so, is certainly laudable, and there is nothing in and of itself wrong with some of the outer rituals, but many outer works are at best unproductive in true spiritual growth, and at worst, can put a person under self condemnation and guilt. The outer rituals can also use up needed time and resources that could be better used in growing in knowledge, wisdom, and understanding.

The primary emphases for each individual should be a cultivation of quiet moments of meditation on spiritual truths and learning to recognize and act upon the internal Voice of God. This Inner Voice leads one to reflect on the great questions we all must answer:

1. Who or What am I?
2. Why am I Here in a Body on Earth?
3. What Exactly IS "God," if God Exists?
4. Since I Innately Seek to Be Free, Must I Accept Death

as Unavoidable and Inevitable Even though My Instinct is to Avoid It?
5. How am I to Know What is True and What is False?
6. A very similar question to the last question is: Can I Know *that* I Know the Truth, about … Any Subject?

A person may know the answer to a question, but if he does not know THAT he knows, he really cannot benefit fully from what he knows. This question also speaks to the idea of whether or not there are limitations as to what we can know. If we are truly limited in what we can know, then how can we believe we will ever be *truly* free?

There are also a lot of other questions an unbibled person may ask, questions that do not require any training in the Bible:

Why do we humans try to escape death? A stone does not appear to try to avoid being crushed or destroyed. Why do we, as well as deer, birds, rabbits, and other life forms, innately experience an urgency to maintain ourselves in our present bodily form without being killed or being eaten by another life form?

Why do our bodies begin to age as early as they do, to some extent sometimes even prior to when we sire or birth children? Why do we not as a species all begin to age at 65 years? Or 80 or 100 years?

Doesn't it seem odd to believe that our body has a life-supporting Intelligence that automatically runs all of our bodily systems, and it causes in us an innate desire to avoid and run away from death, but the same Intelligence provides no alternative but to submit to death? Is it that this Intelligence cannot preserve us, or that something we are doing or not doing affects our ability to be preserved without dying? What is the nature of this Intelligence that enables us to live?

Why do most of us live approximately 70 to 120 years, rather than 500 to 1000, or longer? Of all the billions of people who have ever lived upon the earth, shouldn't statistically at least a small number of the billions live way, way beyond the 70 – 120 years? What forces are at work that prevent us from living without dying?

Why do people "age" at all, rather than simply drop dead without aging?

All of these questions demonstrate that even without religious teachings or culture, it is our nature to ask questions AND seek real, true answers. Seeking answers is an endeavor that occurs because it is our nature to not accept limitation in our understanding. We are not comfortable with ignorance (well, many of us, anyway). We desire to have KNOWING, in order that we may not be limited. We especially chafe against our ignorance that causes us to continue witnessing death putting a limit to our lives in bodily form. If we could, we would also stop our mothers, fathers, family members, friends and others from dying.

For thousands of years, explorers, scientists, leaders and all kinds of people have sought to avoid death -- in its forms of aging, dis-ease, and physically experiencing what we call "dying." Today there are anti-aging creams, anti-aging medical associations, life extension institutes and technology firms offering to make some part of us immortal. The fact of the matter is, whether or not one participates in any of the thousands of religious groups, or disavows any and all religions and doctrines, we all want to avoid dying. Death is distasteful to us. Fear of death grips mankind.

What is the answer? It is to understand the nature of Consciousness and its impact on human genes, tissues, organs, nerves, cells and atoms in the body. Consciousness exerts its impacts whether or not it is understood. It is the flow of Consciousness *through, between, and as* all of the "parts" of our bodies that is key. If the flow is blocked, aging and disease and death result. If the flow is unobstructed, life continues.

The question then becomes: What steps can I take to ensure that the flow of this Consciousness is NOT blocked? This occurs by a change in the way an individual views himself, his body, and everything else in what we call the "universe." The key concept to grasp is that no matter how it appears to our bodily senses, NOTHING in the universe is separate from any (so-called) "other part" of the universe! It is our limited and incomplete senses of seeing, touching, smelling, hearing and tasting that deceive us into believing in separateness between things in our universe. And the only way one can overcome the sense-derived view of separateness is by having a "revelation" (an 'aha' moment of a burst of lighted knowing) about the *connectedness and interpenetration* of everything.

It turns out that "all" is *in* "all." Everything is repeated in and throughout everything "else." In the technological realm, this is beginning to be seen in what man is learning about lasers and holograms.

But not only scientists are awakening to this interconnectedness. Everyday people are waking up. And so can you, the reader of this book ... IF you choose to move beyond knowledge, to wisdom, and beyond wisdom, to understanding ... of the Unity of All Things. The universe is so-designed that experiences of the truth of this will readily come into the lives of those who quietly within themselves determine that they choose to know Reality. We must desire Reality at the cost of forsaking all of our illusions we have believed due to family, cultural, historic and other biases, and of course, the limitations of our senses. Be sure to read the chapter in this book about our senses and "sinning."

So how does an unbibled person conquer and avoid death? In the same way that someone familiar with the bible does: by first desiring to know complete Truth that is not contaminated by even a speck of error. **What part of Truth can we afford NOT to know?** This desire in you for Truth radiates out from within you to all of the universe, and it impacts every atom, molecule, cell and tissue in your body. It also draws or magnetizes into your life experience people and ideas, and new desires. Old habits and ideas will *naturally* fall away from you, in the same way that a leaf falls off a tree quite easily at the right season.

You will find that your hunger for Reality causes a separation to occur in many aspects in your life. Relationships you have may fade as you no longer find commonalities with people who do not possess your thirst to grow in consciousness. You will find that some of your old activities no longer provide enjoyment or satisfaction. Physical possessions become less of an interest, except in how they can be used by you to further your spiritual growth or help others in their growth.

You do not need to immerse yourself in all of the phrases and terminology of the bible, though in some cases, for some people, you may find a growing thirst in you to read and study the scriptures. Abraham heard from God without reading a bible, and he heard very specific instructions as to how to live, where to move to, etc. God's Voice within you does an excellent job of leading you, but it is a growth process, learning how to hear and obey it.

You will see that the Voice inside you grows more certain, and you will find great enjoyment in recognizing this growth. One day this Voice will bear witness to you as to Who you are, in a way that you will know Who and What you have heard. You will understand that what some have called "God" can be better or easier understood to be Cause-That-Is-Everywhere-Present, and that you are one-with Cause and are therefore Cause yourself. Knowing you are *Cause*, that your essence IS Cause, you will choose the quality of your *effects* (experiences) *consciously*.

When you have accomplished all that is in your divine plan for your journey here, you will walk effortlessly into the higher realms. Your mind will have been purified by Truth, and it will have created biochemical benefits in your body, transforming the molecular structure of your body. If you know that your plan includes you taking your transformed body with you, then in a climactic moment, the Fire of Life will consume you and immortalize your body, and you will take your purified body with you as you ascend.

Jesus and Paul referred to death as "sleep." Paul clearly tells us in 1 Corinthians 15:51 that, "We shall not all sleep."

CHAPTER 11

The Conclusion of the Matter

At the end of this book, for those who have read this Message of Life we wish to once again emphasize that it is important to use wisdom in how you respond to the ideas in this writing.

Be wise. Don't do anything stupid. Don't go jumping off a cliff or some other foolish thing to test God or "prove who you are." *When you have achieved everlasting Life, you will have to prove it to no one and you certainly will not act unwisely.*

Obey the daily leading of God's Voice in you. Don't be shocked when some of your most cherished beliefs must be forsaken. Don't quit when the path becomes more challenging than you would have imagined.

You may find it useful to read and re-read this book. Be sure to seek the guidance of the Father Within if you have questions. Know for yourself, because YOU know, not because a group or teacher or someone else you know puts pressure on you to accept what they or society or "experts" and "scholars" say.

If the ideas in this book do not resonate with you, know that we respect you and your right to have your own opinion.

It is sometimes useful to take ideas that you do not

understand or cannot easily digest and figuratively "put them up on the shelf" in your mind. Don't struggle with them, but also do not throw them away or dismiss them entirely if they hold for you some level of interest. Putting them up on the shelf of your mind allows the Father to at another time bring them to your attention and perhaps give you further light on the subject.

Coming here to the earth plane, to live here among others who, like you, are seeking to wake up to Reality, can seem like it is a battle or struggle. Underneath so many of the challenges we encounter is our fear of death, which is basically a fear that our life will be "taken" from us involuntarily. People are afraid that starvation, wars, violence, disease, ignorance, lack, and so many other events and issues may come upon us and take our life, or that if we survive these things, later in a final insult, we still die. So it is understandable why people have tried many methods to delay or avoid death. Unfortunately, unscrupulous people have capitalized on this desire to escape death by selling means and shortcuts offering to stave off death.

There are no shortcuts that work. Overcoming death cannot be "forced" or manipulated, by either well-meaning or ill-intentioned persons. Life can swallow up death in you ONLY by an inner growth of your consciousness. This consciousness IS Life (God) causing you to know for yourself that God/Life alone exists, that you exist IN IT (Acts 17:28), and therefore "you" are IT, and IT is you. When you have realized that there is no more wall of partition between you and everything, then you will be truly free, including free from "death."

If your desire is to choose Life and to be "guided into

ALL Truth," as Jesus promised, you will be guided into all of God (since God IS Truth, and Life), and Truth and Life will be your portion! <u>**When you have come to the place where the work of God has been fully achieved in your life, the Fire of Life will at the Divinely-appointed moment, in the twinkling of an eye, immerse, consume, preserve and transform you, and so shall you ever be with the Lord.**</u>

How could you be guided into ALL Truth and yet still be powerless over death and expect to die?! Being guided into all Truth (John 16:13) is one of the most amazing promises we find in bible! Wouldn't all Truth include knowing how to heal and preserve your body forever? Would you not be one who is described in 1 John 3:9 as a person who *cannot* sin, and therefore not receive the wages or paycheck of sin that is death?

So the conclusion of the matter is this: humbly, with diligence and a clear sense of purpose, seek to understand Life (or differently said, understand Cause or Reality/Truth).

This seeking and finding does not happen overnight. But it DOES happen. You WILL know it when you encounter Life fully. No one will have to tell you it happened, and no one will be able to take it from you.

Whispered inside me came this instruction one day: "If you've got to force it, God does not endorse it." So *allow* yourself to be led and guided by the Divine Voice inside you, what some call the intuition. Be persistent in your seeking to be "guided into ALL Truth," but don't try to force it to happen. Truth never needs to force itself on someone, and Truth cannot be manipulated by the seeker.

"God" (Cause) is everywhere-present. Therefore It can ONLY experience ... Itself. There is nothing outside of Itself to experience! **Right now, Cause is experiencing Itself *as you, the reader, experiencing these words *about Itself*.** And It desires that all who contemplate Itself grow and awaken to the place where they understand that they, too, are Cause -- that you, the reader, are Cause-as-I.

By experiencing your unity with Cause, this will forever change your experiences of your life, which are your *effects* that you, being one-with Cause, create. What kinds of experiences do you choose to experience?

God said in Deuteronomy 28:13 that if we follow His leading, he would make us "the head and not the tail" – meaning, we will remember ourselves as one-with Cause, rather than see ourselves in the seemingly separate realm of effect.

The greatest gift you will encounter as you allow the work of God to eliminate senses-derived erroneous thinking in you is the gift of Peace. True Knowledge, what the bible calls the "Knowledge of the Holy" IS Peace. It is Peace from knowing that there exists ONLY One Power, which is Cause. This Peace *lasts* -- and the benefits are profound for your mind (your body of knowledge) and your physical body.

As the apostle Paul penned in 1 Corinthians 15:26, your last enemy that will be destroyed is death. We read in verses 51-54 that "we shall not all sleep" (die), but we shall all be changed ... (when) this corruptible (mind) shall have put on incorruption, and this mortal (body) shall have put on immortality, then (FOR YOU) shall be brought to pass the saying … death (your last enemy) is swallowed up in victory." This is a fulfillment of the words in Isaiah 25:8, that "He will swallow up death in victory."

Connecting with Others Who Resonate with This Message, and Supporting Its Spread

If this Message brings in you an inner joy and certainty, and a gratitude for the Light manifested in you by this writing, if you would like to fellowship with others who are like-minded, visit the website www.dontinsistondying.org. Or you may visit: www.pioneerinsights.org. Correspondence may also be sent by mail to: Pioneer Place Ministries Inc. P.O. Box 1051 Ellijay GA 30540 USA. As we are able, we also hope to make information available through social media platforms, but you may wish to look on both traditional and non-traditional platforms.

Please note that gifts are gratefully accepted, but Pioneer Place Ministries is not a "nonprofit" 501c3 public charity and therefore gifts are not tax deductible. Nothing God does happens without "profit" (meaning, spiritual growth, in wisdom and understanding). So we are not interested in any part of this work being "nonprofit." Funds received will be used to further the spread of this Message. If you have skills, connections, technologies or resources that would assist in the dissemination of this Word of Life, please feel free to send us a note.

A Culture of Life, Not Death

And God shall wipe away all tears from their eyes; and there shall be **no more death**, neither sorrow, nor crying, neither shall there be any more pain: for **the former things are passed away**.

—Revelation 21:4

It is time now for a culture of Life to manifest in the earth realm, replacing the culture of death with its mindset of limitation and lack, festivals of death, abortions, production and eating of meat, and glorification of force and violence. As this bible verse says, death must become a "former thing," and who better to manifest this than you and I?

Understanding is a wellspring of life unto him that hath it.

—Proverbs 16:22

For with Thee is the fountain of life: in Thy light shall we see light.

—Psalms 36:9

www.ingramcontent.com/pod-product-compliance
Lightning Source LLC
Chambersburg PA
CBHW072101290426
44110CB00014B/1770